Praise From the First Mosaic Group

"This study has given me a Godly outlook on what it looks like to follow Jesus and struggle with mental health. It's helped me hone in on God's voice and what He says about me instead of what others say. It has also made me realize that the pain I'm feeling is also felt by God and He has never left me for one second."

– Leigha Turner, University of Georgia

"Conversations surrounding faith and mental health are always hard and sometimes awkward, however, going through this course I realized it doesn't have to be that way. I have always felt ashamed to admit that I struggle with mental health issues as a Christian, but I was reassured through this material that these two things can coexist. I now feel equipped to move through life with the knowledge I have gained and I move forward very excited that so many more people are going to have the same opportunity to experience growth and connection."

– Sydney LaBollita, University of Georgia

"I am someone who has struggled with mental health issues since before I can remember. Anxiety has always felt like the most powerful and unshakable truth in my life, and depression pushed me further into hopelessness and exhaustion. But this is not the truth. The Lord, His sacrifice, and His love for each and every one of us is the ultimate truth and in being a part of this Bible study, my belief in this truth has only grown. This is the first time in a church setting that I have gotten the chance to examine deeply and speak vulnerably of the reality of my experiences with mental health in a space that is open and with people who understand because they have been through it, too. I am so thankful to have gotten to study Cam's insight into how God's word reveals his character towards those who feel lost and tired and scared. I will cherish this study to remember I am never alone in my struggles, and that the Lord my God is there for me always."

-Riley McNeill, University of Georgia

Mosaic

Renewing Your Mental Health with God

Cameron Pace

Briley & Baxter Publications | Plymouth, Massachusetts

ISBN: 978-1-954819-69-6

Book Design: Eleonor Gardner

To the people that were
outcasted by the church because of
their struggles with mental health.

To the people who are struggling
and looking for more.

To the people who are just trying
to understand what their loved ones
are going through.

This is for you.

"Let us draw near to God with a sincere heart and with the full assurance that faith brings, having our hearts sprinkled to cleanse us from a guilty conscience and having our bodies washed with pure water. Let us hold unswervingly to the hope we profess, for he who promised is faithful. And let us consider how we may spur one another on toward love and good deeds, not giving up meeting together, as some are in the habit of doing, but encouraging one another—and all the more as you see the Day approaching."

—Hebrews 10: 22-25 NIV

Table of Contents

Foreword

To say I am excited for you is an understatement. You are holding this book in your hands because you are, at bare minimum, intrigued by the intersection of mental health and God. And at most, you are desperate for a breakthrough for yourself or for someone you love. I'm so proud of you and hopeful for the journey you are about to embark on.

Cam and I met in Spring 2022 at More, the UGA Wesley Foundation's annual mental health event. I was invited to be the guest speaker and Cam was an organizer and panelist at the event. One thing that struck me from that first meeting was Cam's authenticity and openness with her mental health journey. She is sharing not just for others to know this part of her story, but also to allow them to learn and benefit from it as well. She does not come from the unrelatable place of "having it all figured out," but reads as just a few steps further on the path and invites you to grab hold of the treasure, skills, and tools she has already discovered.

What you will find in this book are research-based practices and techniques, with their foundation primarily in Cognitive Behavioral Therapy (CBT), and an integration of Solution-Focused Brief Therapy (SFBT) and other techniques as well. CBT is one of the most commonly practiced theoretical orientations in psychotherapy and is especially effective in alleviating anxiety and depression. CBT is often viewed as a highly concrete and practical theory in which thought patterns can actually be changed, which in turn influences beliefs, feelings, and behaviors.

Far from being a highly clinical and inaccessible textbook, this Bible study reads much more like a friendly guidebook as you take steps in your mental health journey. Cam teaches readers basic therapeutic skills that they can apply right now to take a reflective look at their own mental health, thought patterns, and practices. If they find there is a thought pattern that is not serving them well or yielding the kind of fruit they desire, she seamlessly integrates scripture throughout this study to allow them to find a more life-giving way.

If you are typically more of an independent learner and grower, can I encourage you for a moment? This study can be used that way; however, it was intended for you to work through with a small group. Why? Not to expose you, but to empower you. There is this amazing thing that happens when you are authentic and vulnerable enough to say the "hard thing" to a trusted person(s). Through this group study, not only are you allowing God to search and know you in a new way, but you are also bringing things into the light (Ephesians 5:13) with people. If that feels too risky, consider this—we don't know what we don't know. When it comes to our own thoughts, there is often much that we have a hard time really knowing until we share it in community. Oftentimes, we are so entrenched in our own minds and so accustomed to how we think in our own internal dialogue, that we don't really know any other way.

In my six years as a high school counselor and current clinical work at a non-profit counseling agency, I am allowed firsthand privilege of how vital these tools and skills are to clients as they walk in their process. There is no shortcut to freedom. To promise one would be folly. However, the skills Cam teaches and facilitates will produce a harvest in due time as they are practiced diligently, empowered by the Spirit, within the context of community.

That is my prayer for you, reader—that through this Bible study, as you learn and practice new tools (or just tools you haven't brought out of the shed in a while) you would see change empowered by the Spirit who leads you from glory to glory. And that you would do the whole thing in the context of people, that they may call out the gold they see in you, and lift you up when your foot stumbles. Amen.

LORA PITNER, M.ED.

God takes the pieces of us that we see as broken and redeems them with His love, turning our broken pieces into a beautiful mosaic. He can transform the mess into a masterpiece.

Before We Get Started

Introduction

Along the path of healing, many of us have wrestled with questions, such as: Is this struggle/diagnosis who I am? Has God left me? Is this all God has in His plan for me? Does this mean God loves me less? The good news is the answer to each of these questions is no. Your circumstances, diagnosis(es), and past actions do not define you. God is still right by your side working all things together for your good. He doesn't love you any less.

Many of us who struggle with mental health feel that some part of us is broken. We feel incomplete and flawed because of the things we struggle with. The pieces of ourselves that we see as broken and worthless do not appear that way to God. We see ourselves as if we are broken glass scattered all over the floor; a mess that cannot be put back together just like we were before. Where we see a mess, God sees the makings of a masterpiece, and throughout our lives, He turns our pieces into something new— a mosaic comprised by each unique piece of us. Oftentimes, we are surprised when healing changes us, but that's the whole point. We're not supposed to stay the same! As we walk through life with God, we're going to be transformed. We're going to be changed. God takes the pieces of us that we see as broken and redeems them with His love, turning our broken pieces into a beautiful mosaic. He can transform the mess into a masterpiece.

My Testimony

You may be wondering what gives me the qualifications to write this book. I'm not a pastor or a licensed therapist, I'm a seminary student (as of this writing) who is still trying to figure out this whole adulthood thing. However, this book is a compilation of the insights of pastors, therapists, doctors, and nurses, that I have met during this healing journey. This book is a compilation of what brought me out of the darkest pits a human being can find themselves in. **This book is full of things that have been proven to work.** I want to tell you my story so that you can see all that is possible for you.

My name is Cameron Pace, and I am a University of Georgia alum, UGA Wesley employee, and a student at Asbury Theological Seminary. I have struggled with depression, anxiety, and suicidal ideation (SI) all of my life.

The earliest memories I have of wanting to take my own life date all the way back to my 6th-grade year when I was 11 years old. I've always been the shy kid who was scared to open up and talk, leading me to a place of extreme loneliness. My loneliness, combined with struggling academically, was the formation of a storm cloud I've had floating over me ever since. Throughout middle and high school these feelings persisted. Over the course of those years, I wrote more than five letters with the intent of saying goodbye, but (thank God) I was never able to follow through.

I had grown up in the church but felt as though God had left me because of everything I was going through. I wasn't sure how the "good God" they described on Sundays could exist when I was struggling so much. I went to church every Sunday, much to my dismay, but sat with a heart that was cold, closed off, and hard. After my senior year of high school, I went to the church retreat that I had attended throughout my middle and high school career, but something was different. Contrary to how in the past I felt detached and distant, I felt connected, not only to my peers, but to God as well. I experienced God's presence for the first time the summer before my freshman year of college, and during that week the Lord met me and completely transformed my life. I was happy for the first time I could remember and I began to carry myself as a child of God should. I cannot tell you what was different at this retreat versus all the ones I had been to in the past, but there is not a doubt in my mind that, despite growing up in church, that was the moment God saved me.

Unfortunately, instead of using this momentum from my breakthrough with God to begin healing the parts of my heart and mind that had been negatively impacted by mental illness, I pretended that the parts didn't exist at all. I would not let God or anyone else into those parts of my life because I was embarrassed and believed that if I ignored my struggles they would go away. This didn't work and in my sophomore year of college I became plagued by panic attacks day and night; I was never rested and I was scared all the time. When COVID-19 hit and the world shut down, disconnecting me from my friends and every other distraction in my life, I began to spiral and my anxiety and depression took me over. I began having multiple panic attacks a day and would feel as though I was never good enough.

Later that same year I began to go to therapy, and my life began to change. I was actually processing everything going on in my head and all I was feeling. After several months in therapy with little decrease in the panic attacks, my counselor and I realized that my anxiety and depression were not only caused by trauma I had endured but were most likely caused by a chemical imbalance as well. I decided to visit my physician, which is where I took the Screen for Adult Anxiety Related Disorders (SCAARED); the highest possible score someone could get on this exam is an 88, which would mean experiencing all 44 symptoms very often. I scored a 62, making it clear that I needed extra help. I began to take medication shortly after my exam and after trying several medication combinations, paired with therapy, my panic attacks ceased, my depression waned, and I could finally function again.

However, my heart still felt dark. At the time I was in a long-term relationship with someone I cared about deeply, but he and I were in different stages in life and had different morals. With my college graduation quickly approaching, I was ready to begin thinking about the future, but he just wanted to have fun and focus on the present. I wanted to make the relationship work so badly that I ignored God and tried to make it work for another half a year. After lots of wrestling with God, I finally ended the relationship, and he and I went our separate ways. I loved him very deeply and the pain from the breakup was more than I could bear, but much of my anxiety dissipated and I began to feel better. I began to realize that I had been leaning on my ex more than I was relying on God, so I began to channel most of my energy toward God again.

Several weeks later I found out about lies I had been told throughout the relationship and that he had been unfaithful. And this, paired with the pain of the breakup and other problems occurring in my personal life, pushed me over the edge. I had thoughts of SI and had hurt myself emotionally through self-sabotaging behaviors, and physically many times before. But I wanted it to be the last time so I decided to admit myself to an inpatient psychiatric facility where I spent a week learning about much of this book's contents.

After my discharge, I returned to Athens, GA for my final semester of college, happier and healthier than I had ever been. I continue to work with my counselor and still have ups and downs and loopy loops, but I am processing it all with God and using the tools I've written down for you in this book. I don't know how many people will read this book, but I do know that things God has revealed to me are too good to keep to myself. I believe that when the practices in this book are applied to your own life, you will begin to experience healing, and through inviting Him into the process you'll grow closer to God. I have seen healing and deeper intimacy in my life and the lives of my friends who have read this book, and I want the same good things for you.

Let's dive in.

Foundations

Week 1: Introductions

Week 2: Who You Say I Am

Week 3: Cornerstone

Week 1: Introductions

I don't know anything about what kind of group you're taking this journey with—whether you've known each other your whole lives or if you're just meeting for the first time. However, I do know the journey we are about to embark on together is deep and will have us face some of our biggest struggles and insecurities. You want to embark on a journey like this with people you know, so this first week will be solely devoted to learning about those in your group.

First, fill out the Who Am I chart on the next page. Share your answers with the group. It's okay if you leave some boxes blank!

Next, I'm going to ask you to share your testimony. For some of you, this may be really scary. Others may have done it a thousand times. For all, I know this could be your first time meeting one another, so I'm not asking you to bare your soul and lay all your cards on the table. I want to challenge you to share what I call a two-minute testimony. A two-minute testimony is made up of three parts: "before God I," "I met God when," and "because of God now I." Sharing your testimonies with one another allows you to get to know each other more deeply, but also requires transparency and vulnerability—two skills that are vital to engaging in this study.

You have already read my testimony and know it is full of a LOT, and I'm going to show you how I would condense it for this exercise:

Goals	Talents	Passions

I've always wanted to...	WHO AM I?	Spiritual Gifts

Hobbies	Role Models	I want to grow in...

Before God, depression and anxiety ruled my life, and I didn't think life had a point. **I met God when** I went on a youth retreat the summer before my freshman year of college. **Because of God, now I** am walking in freedom, continuing to grow and I'm building my relationship with Him.

See?! Easy! I could share this with any person I meet and I know it would not overwhelm them or me. **Now you try. Write your two-minute testimony below, and share it with the group.**

1. Before God I…

2. I met God when…

3. Because of God now I…

During this time, I'm asking you to do one of the bravest things a person can do: let the people in this group truly know you. Don't lie and say you're doing great when you aren't. Don't act a certain way just because it's what you think people want. No fronts, no facades, just an authentic you. To do this takes courage and vulnerability. It takes a lot, but for your own good and your own healing, I am asking you to take this leap of faith. **Answer these questions 100% truthfully. Be bold. Share!**

1. What brought you to this group?

2. How would you describe your current starting point?

3. What are you hoping to get out of this group?

4. Is there anything the group can help hold you accountable for?

Wrapping Up

Throughout this next week pray to God to give you boldness so you can open yourself up to those around you. Pray for trust in the work the Lord will be doing during this time.

Week 2: Who You Say I Am

Check-In Question:

Rate how you are feeling mentally, emotionally, and spiritually on a scale of 1-10 (10 being great, 1 being awful).

Read Judges 6: 1-18

Reflect

Imagine being in Gideon's place: hiding away in a small cramped space for safety, scared to get hurt. While we are not hiding from Midianites who threaten to steal our food and land, we often hide away from the things that are intended to hurt us, and in our fear, we lose the sense of who we truly are. Fear is debilitating because it can be so defining for us when we lose sight of the Lord. Fear makes us question things we know to be true and leads us to be terrified of the unknown. Fear is at the root of the many lies we hear in our minds; lies that say we are not good enough, that we are defined by what we struggle with, that we are unloved.

Gideon believes himself to be weak and incapable and yet God greets him by saying, "'The Lord is with you, mighty warrior.'"[1] One of the most amazing things about God is that what we believe about ourselves never prevents Him from seeing us as we truly are. Even in the moments where we cannot see the good in ourselves God always can, no matter what our circumstances may be. He not only sees our true nature, He sees our greatest potential and all we are capable of. Even when hearing his true identity spoken over him straight from the mouth of God, Gideon still doubts that he is capable of doing what the Lord has called him to, and in his doubt, he asks God to give him a sign that he has truly found favor in the Lord's eyes. Instead

---

1 Judges 6:12

11

of chastising Gideon, the Lord responds with, "I will wait for your return."[2] We are so blessed to have a God who waits for us even in our moments of doubt.

It is easy to let the things of this world define us, whether it be by our possessions, achievements, or our friend group. It is very easy for us to feel as if our mental health struggles or diagnoses define us when we're basing our identity on our circumstances rather than the truths that God says about us.

What have you been letting define you? Where is your self-worth coming from?

_____

_____

_____

_____

_____

_____

_____

_____

_____

_____

_____

_____

_____

_____

_____

_____

_____

_____

_____

2 Judges 6:18

Each of us wrestle with allowing fear and this world to define us, and yet we serve a God who has already revealed our true identity and is just waiting for us to step into who He has made us to be. He has created us exactly how He wants us to be.

List 5 things you like about how God made you:

1.

2.

3.

4.

5.

When lies are planted in our minds we must fight them with God's truth. Use the table to answer these questions.

What are three statements from this list that you do believe?

1.

2.

3.

What are three statements from this list that you want to believe?

1.

2.

3.

Who He Says I Am...	Where He Says It...
I am wonderfully made.	Psalm 139:14
I am God's friend.	John 15:15
I am chosen and loved by God.	Colossians 3:12
I am adopted into His family.	Romans 8:15
I am a child of God.	John 1:12
I am not a slave to sin through Christ's sacrifice.	Romans 6:6
I am accepted as I am.	Romans 15:7
I am made new, and my past doesn't define me.	2 Corinthians 5:17
I am set free.	Galatians 5:1
I am seated with Christ in heavenly places.	Ephesians 2:6
I am transformed, refined, and sanctified by God.	2 Corinthians 3:18

It is so important for us to speak and declare these truths over ourselves. The words we think and speak over ourselves have great weight in how we view our identities. We are told in Proverbs that the power of life and death is in the tongue[3], so when we speak about ourselves we are either speaking life over ourselves or death. This is why it is so important for us to say good things about ourselves and to speak the truths that God has provided us with. When we speak the truths that God has said about us we are using the power of our words to build ourselves up, instead of giving power to the enemy and allowing his lies to tear us down.

The enemy wants to distort our view of who the Lord has created us to be because if we are not confident in who God has made us be we will not be confident enough to walk into the calling that He has for us. We have to take God at His word and believe that how he identifies us is true.

What are some of the lies about yourself the enemy tries to convince you of? What truths from the chart above can you use to combat these lies?

_____

_____

_____

---

3 Proverbs 18:21

_____

_____

_____

_____

_____

_____

_____

_____

"Then God said, 'Let us make mankind in our image, in our likeness, so that they may rule over the fish in the sea and the birds in the sky, over the livestock and all the wild animals, and over all the creatures that move along the ground.'

So God created mankind in his own image,

in the image of God he created them;

male and female he created them."

—Genesis 1: 26-27

Each and every one of us is made in the image of the Lord Almighty. Even when we cannot believe that we are loved and worthy we can know that we carry the greatest honor of all: being an image-bearer for the King of Kings. In order to be true image-bearers, we must be familiar with God's character.

What are the qualities of God? What qualities of God are apparent in you?

_____

_____

_____

_____

_____

_____

_____

As God's image-bearers, we were made to reflect God and His character to the people around us. To be true reflections of the King we need to become less like who we see as the ideal version of ourselves and more like the version of ourselves God intended for us to be.

Take a moment and sit in prayer. Ask God who He made you to be. Let go of your own expectations of yourself and write what He tells you.

_____

_____

_____

_____

_____

_____

_____

_____

_____

_____

_____

_____

_____

_____

_____

_____

_____

_____

Fill out the Who Am I chart and leave no boxes blank. Share if there are any differences in your answers.

Wrapping Up

Over the next week, post the facts that God has said to you where you can see them, so that you may be reminded of them daily. Pray that you go from knowing that it is true, to believing that it is true. I know about Santa Clause, but I don't *believe* in Santa Clause. In the same way, I can know these things about myself without believing them.

Week 3: Cornerstone

Check-In Question:

Over the past week, how has the Lord revealed your true identity to you? How has walking in the identity God has created for you changed your day-to-day life? Discuss.

Read Matthew 7:24-29, 1 Corinthians 3:10-13, Genesis 2:1-3

Reflect

Multiple times in scripture we are called to have the Lord as our foundation—to build our whole life upon him—but what does this mean? Our life is built on whatever we revolve our life around. For many, their lives are built on and revolve around school, work, or relationships.

What does your life currently revolve around?

_____

_____

_____

_____

_____

_____

_____

_____

_____

_____

_____

_____

_____

Like the sand in the parable of the wise and foolish builders, anything that is not God can shift with a gust of wind. If we build our lives on things that are ever-changing, our lives will be volatile and in constant turmoil. The Lord does not want this for us, and God gave us Himself as a foundation so we would not have to live that way.

God is the only thing in the universe that is truly constant and unchanging; we are told in Hebrews 13 that "Jesus Christ is the same yesterday and today and tomorrow." When our lives are built on something constant, even when the world around us is a mess we can stand firm and feel secure like those who built their house on rock. When our lives are built on school, something as small as a bad grade can poison our entire outlook. However, if God is our foundation our outlook is never poisoned in this way because He is always good, He is always in control, and He is always kind.

But how do we build our lives upon God? We can't see Him or touch Him, but we can invest in our relationship with Him by making Him our first priority in our schedules. Instead of fitting God into the leftover parts of your day, schedule your time with Him first and fit everything else around it. Let's take a minute to assess our schedules. It's easy to look at our busy schedules and packed Google calendars and feel like we have no time. In today's culture that tells us we have to "hustle" or "grind" to be important, packing our schedules to the brim with activities is glorified.

What does your typical day look like? Be honest! Include time on social media, watching tv, etc.

	Sunday	Monday	Tuesday	Wednesday	Thursday	Friday	Saturday
Morning							
Afternoon							
Night							

Look at your schedule. About how much time do you currently spend with God in your day-to-day life?

_____

_____

_____

_____

_____

_____

_____

_____

_____

_____

What areas lose time when you become overwhelmed and stressed?

_____

_____

_____

_____

_____

_____

_____

_____

_____

How can you shift your schedule to make time with God the first priority?

_____

_____

_____

_____

_____

_____

_____

_____

_____

_____

Managing our time well is one of the ways we can make God the foundation of our lives. One of the ways we can spend our time with God is in His word. Spending time in our Bibles makes us closer to God because "all scripture is God-breathed" meaning it is from God himself. By familiarizing ourselves with scripture we begin to know the heart and character of God and can reflect it in our own lives.

How much time do you typically spend in the word?
(There is no shame in answering this question honestly! I will be the first to say that I am not always in scripture as much as I should be!)

_____

_____

_____

_____

What typically keeps you from spending time in scripture?

_____

_____

_____

_____

_____

_____

_____

_____

_____

_____

Genesis 2 verse 3 tells us that <u>because God rested on the seventh day it was made holy.</u> Let me repeat that. The days where God spoke the whole earth into being were not deemed holy, the day he _rested_ was deemed holy. We were not made to be all go nonstop, and God makes this clear in His model for how we should live. God would not highlight and model rest if it were not so important for us; God cares about how we spend our time.

In the hustle and bustle of our lives, Sunday very easily can become our catch-up day: laundry, chores, grocery shopping, homework, and so forth. You name it, and it can probably go on that list. This is not the way God has called us to live. It is important for us to observe the Sabbath weekly. God took the time to model for us the appropriate rhythms of work and rest: 6 days working and 1 day resting. On the Sabbath, we are called to focus our eyes on the Lord and nothing else.

What are things you can do on the sabbath to focus on and honor God?

_____

_____

_____

_____

_____

_____

_____

_____

_____

How can you rearrange your schedule to ensure that you observe the sabbath?

_____

_____

_____

_____

_____

_____

_____

_____

_____

_____

Wrapping Up

Here are some goals you can be reaching for this week:

- Find a Bible reading plan and commit to it

- Make God your first priority every day

- Find friends you can read the Word with. When will you meet with God this week?

Together

Week 4: In the Valley

Check-In Question:

How have you been leaning on God as your foundation this past week?

Read Genesis 16:1-14

Reflect

God promised Abram and Sarai a child, but in the waiting they got impatient. As a result, Hagar was forced to have a child with Abram; Hagar didn't get to make the choice, the choice was made for her by Sarai. However, even though Hagar did exactly what Sarai wanted, Sarai turned bitter and jealous toward her. After being dealt with so harshly, Hagar flees. Think of Hagar's circumstances: she was a pregnant, unwed slave. She held no place in society and would have been looked down upon. She was stripped of her control. She was alone. She had nowhere to go. In a moment where she could not have possibly felt more helpless and invisible, God encountered her. The woman that the rest of the world had turned their backs on was still deemed worthy by God. God not only saw her where she was, but He also listened to her pain (verse 11) and told her how He would redeem it (verse 12).

God sees us as we are, even in the midst of our struggle, just like He saw Hagar out in the desert. At the lowest point of Hagar's life, God still saw her; He is *El Roi*, "the God who sees me." He is with us regardless of our circumstances, and throughout His Word, we are reminded time and time again that He is always with us.

Are there times when you have felt like God left you? What made Him feel far away?

_____

_____

_____

_____

_____

_____

_____

_____

_____

In our most difficult moments, it is easy to forget that God is still near. We struggle with how a good God could let bad things happen to the people He loves. God doesn't force bad things upon us; that is the consequence of living among sin in a fallen world, but in His loving kindness He uses bad things for good: "And we know that in all things God works for the good of those who love Him, who have been called according to His purpose." The enemy tries to attack us by placing negative thoughts about God in our minds, and we often wonder why we have to go through these things: why we struggle with mental illness/ someone we love does, the loss of a loved one, the end of a relationship, getting overlooked. Instead of asking the "why" behind the circumstance, we need to ask the "what" and "how."

- What is God trying to teach me right now?

- How has He been good to me despite my circumstances?

- What is He putting on my heart during this time?

- How can I use this for God's glory?

I believe the biggest "why" many people struggling with their mental health is the following: "God, I have prayed and I'm doing everything I'm supposed to. Why won't you take this from me? Does this mean you don't love me?" I have found these questions incredibly apparent in my own life, but my counselor pointed out something to me that changed my life and how I view my circumstances.

Oftentimes we claim to be praying for healing when in reality we're praying for something else entirely. Healing is a process. There are ups and downs and loopy loops, so when we pray for healing we should invite God into that process. However, many of us don't actually want to go through the process, we just want the pain to be gone. When we pray for healing but expect the complete eradication of a struggle in an instant, we are praying for healing with the expectation of a miracle instead of a process. God is completely capable of miracles, but it is unfair for us to be frustrated when we pray for healing and are instead greeted by a process and not an instantaneous change. Furthermore, just because God can perform miracles of healing, does not necessarily mean that is what He has in store for us in our own stories. Miracles can happen, but the absence of one does not mean God loves you any less. Paul, one of the most prominent apostles and biblical teachers ever, is a great example of this. In 2 Corinthians 12, Paul tells us:

> *"Even if I should choose to boast, I would not be a fool, because I would be speaking the truth. But I refrain, so no one will think more of me than is warranted by what I do or say, or because of these surpassingly great revelations. Therefore, in order to keep me from becoming conceited, I was given a thorn in my flesh, a messenger of Satan, to torment me. Three times I pleaded with the Lord to take it away from me."*

There is no doubt in any of our minds that God loved Paul. If we look at Paul and know God didn't remove the thorn in his side, despite God's love for him, why do we believe that the absence of a miracle is a reflection of God's lack of love for us?

Life with God was never promised to be easy and pain-free; life with God promises His presence and love. Your circumstances are not a reflection of how much God loves you. The circumstances surrounding your mental illness are not caused by a lack of faith on your part. We all have weaknesses; Paul had a thorn in his side, and he most likely struggled with it his whole life. When Paul asked for the thorn to be taken away, God's response to Paul was:

> *"But He said to me, 'My grace is sufficient for you, for my power is made perfect in weakness.' Therefore I will boast all the more gladly about my weaknesses, so that Christ's power may rest on me. "*

Through our weaknesses, we get to partner with God, and through our weaknesses, God's power is made perfect. Hear me: WE ARE PARTNERING WITH THE CREATOR OF EVERYTHING AND WE CAN BE PART OF SHOWCASING HIS PERFECT POWER! Do you all realize how CRAZY that is?! Not only do we get the opportunity to partner with God, but we also get to glorify God through our weaknesses. If we could do everything in our own strength we wouldn't need God, but doing things that are only possible with God highlights how great and good He is!

Our whole lives are an act of worship, and I can't think of a better way to worship than to be a living sacrifice and allow God to move through your weaknesses however He wants to. When we love God and are obedient, not only does He work for His glory but He works for our good as well. Romans 8:28 tells says, "And we know that in all things God works for the good of those who love Him, who have been called according to his purpose."

Look back on your life. How have you seen God make good out of the low points of your life?

_____

_____

_____

_____

_____

_____

_____

_____

_____

Wrapping Up

Over the next few weeks, make time to sit with God and ask Him to help you answer the following questions. Listen for His voice and allow Him to open your eyes to the good He is making out of the bad.

- What is God trying to teach me right now?

- How has He been good to me despite my circumstances?

- What is He putting on my heart in this time?

- How can I use this for God's glory?

- Be ready to share all the good God has done when we next meet!

Week 5: Breaking Down the Walls

Check-In Question:

Over the past week, how have you seen God's goodness when dealing with hard things? Discuss.

Read Mark 4:35-41

Reflect

The storm is not just any old storm, it is a squall, "a sudden violent gust of wind or storm." Imagine you're in a tiny little boat: the waves are smacking the sides, the wind is pushing you to and fro, you can feel the boat start to tip and it doesn't but you feel like it will. You begin to panic, and you wonder how Jesus could possibly be sleeping at a time like this! The storm was a particularly stressful moment for the disciples.

How can you relate to the disciples and how they feel in this stressful moment?

_____

_____

_____

_____

_____

_____

_____

_____

_____

_____

_____

_____

In life, our stress and stressors can act as our own personal squalls. We may not experience squalls every day, but we do experience stressful moments every day.

How has stress affected your day-to-day life?

_____

_____

_____

_____

_____

_____

_____

_____

_____

_____

_____

_____

_____

_____

_____

Identifying our triggers is the first step in not letting our stress or negative thoughts/feelings control us! Triggers, also called stressors, are physical and/or social circumstances that cause the release of stress hormones, hindering our ability to adapt; they are what send us down a tunnel of anxiety[4].

What are some of the stressors that can trigger you in your day-to-day life? List them and put a star next to the triggers that cause you the most stress.

_____

_____

_____

_____

_____

_____

_____

_____

_____

_____

Below, think of 3 stressful moments you typically encounter in your daily routine. Write how you typically react:

1.

_____

4 _Stressors_. Centre For Studies on Human Stress (CSHS). (2017, August 22). Retrieved April 12, 2022, from https://humanstress.ca/stress/what-is-stress/stressors/#:~:text=A%20stressor%20is%20anything%20that,physical)%20stressors%20and%20Psychological%20Stressor

American Psychological Association. (n.d.). _APA Dictionary of Psychology: Stressors_. American Psychological Association. Retrieved April 12, 2022, from https://dictionary.apa.org/stressor

2.

3.

Some stresses can cause us to spiral and cause us to engage in **negative coping skills** (handling our problems in a way that hurts us). The thoughts that lead to those strategies are often rooted in the lie that Christ, or people in general, just don't care. Do not let this lie win! The most important part of the story is that when the disciples turned to Christ, <u>He calmed the storm.</u>

When we are rooted in Christ, we have the gift of experiencing his peace, and we can take action by engaging in **positive coping skills** (handling our problems in a way that helps us). Negative coping skills are walls we have built up in the past to protect ourselves, but as we let God into the process we break these walls down and focus on helping ourselves instead of just avoiding potential hurt. We create coping strategies to help us survive our greatest stressors; **identify the positive and negative coping skills you currently use.**

Positive Skills	Negative Skills
☒ Take your medication consistently* ☒ Make a list or journal about what you are thankful for ☒ Create a balanced schedule ☒ Start or revisit a hobby ☒ Exercise ☒ Therapy* ☒ Grounding Techniques* ☒ Say a prayer ☒ Spend time with people who uplift you ☒ Watch a feel-good movie or TV show ☒ Games and puzzles ☒ Take a warm shower or bath ☒ Read your Bible	☒ Self-harm (cutting, scratching; hurting yourself) ☒ Lashing out at others ☒ Oversleeping or not sleeping enough ☒ Overeating or avoiding eating ☒ Self-hate/negative self-talk (thinking "I'm worthless," "I'm stupid," etc.) ☒ Expressing anger by yelling ☒ Distancing yourself from loved ones ☒ Physically harming others ☒ Intentionally avoiding work ☒ Drinking or taking drugs ☒ Suicidal Ideation (SI)

For more info check out the More & More section

Recall your answers to how you would respond to 3 stressful moments you typically encounter. Would you respond any differently after reading the different types of positive and negative coping skills?

_____

_____

_____

_____

_____

_____

_____

_____

_____

_____

_____

_____

How can you invite God into dealing with your stress?

_____

_____

_____

_____

_____

_____

_____

_____

Wrapping Up

Positive coping skills are great, but remember there is nothing greater than turning to Christ in times of stress. Spend time in the word, sit with Him in prayer, journal, write yourself a letter from God to you; however, you best connect with God, do it!

As a way to visualize the progress you've made, in the space below, write down the moments throughout the week where you chose a positive coping skill when you typically would have chosen a negative one!

Week 6: People Need People

Check-In Question:

How has your prayer life changed over the past week? What new ways did you connect with God?

Read John 15: 12-13, 17:20-23

Reflect

Not only are we instructed to love our neighbors, but it is also God's 2nd GREATEST commandment to us! God's heart for His people is to be in community with one another and to build relationships that reflect God's love.

How would you describe your community? Do they reflect God's love? Do you reflect God's love for them?

_____

_____

_____

_____

_____

_____

_____

_____

_____

_____

_____

_____

_____

Are there areas of your life you are cautious to share with your community? Why?

_____

_____

_____

_____

_____

_____

_____

_____

_____

_____

_____

_____

_____

Even in the very beginning, mankind was not called good until Adam was in community with Eve. When looking back at God's original design, it is clear that God's true intention for us is to live in community with other believers. Establishing a community and experiencing God's love through others is one of life's sweetest gifts.

It is key for us to have people in our lives we can lean on and talk to. Notice I say lean; we can ask our friends for help and talk to them when we are struggling, but they are not intended to take God's place as your foundation. When we try to stand on our relationships and we put on too much pressure, the relationship crumbles. God is who you stand on, you can find everything you'll ever need in Him. Having community as God intended can give us support in trying seasons.

Think of your friends, who would you consider "safe" people to talk to when you are struggling?

_____

_____

_____

_____

_____

_____

_____

_____

What qualities make this person safe?

_____

_____

_____

_____

_____

_____

_____

To ensure we aren't putting too much pressure on our relationships we need to be aware of our boundaries. Boundaries allow us to honor ourselves and the people we are in a relationship with. Generally speaking, there are three types of boundaries[5]:

Rigid Boundaries	Healthy Boundaries	Porous Boundaries
• Avoids close relationships and intimacy/ few close friendships • Distances themselves from others to avoid rejection • Typically will not ask for help • Overly protective about their personal information • Detached	• Values their own opinions • Will not compromise values for others • Shares personal information appropriately (not over/under sharing) • Knows their wants and needs, and is able to communicate them • Able to accept "no" from others	• Overshares personal information • Has trouble saying "no" • Overinvolved with the problems of others • Dependent on the opinions of others • Accepts abuse and disrespect • Fears they will be rejected if they don't do what others want

Which type sounds the most like you?

_____

_____

_____

_____

Not every person in our life needs to know the details of what we're going through, and that's part of why setting boundaries is so important! Let's take the time to map out your support system.

Fill out this list with the names of people who fit the prompt.

▪ Someone I can discuss my problems with:

▪ Someone who enjoys the same activities:

▪ Someone who can cheer me up:

▪ Someone who builds my self-confidence

5 Spiese, E. (2019, April 12). *Understanding Boundaries*. Anxiety & Stress Center, P.C. Retrieved April 12, 2022, from https://anxiety-stresscenter.com/understanding-boundaries/#:~:text=Individuals%20with%20rigid%20boundaries%20often,and%20allow%20for%20inappropriate%20interactions.

- Someone who will give me wise advice:

- Someone who is a good listener:

- Someone who can help when I'm sick:

- Someone who can hold me accountable:

- Someone who can be honest with me about my mistakes:

- Someone who mentors me:

Hopefully, after 6 weeks of walking this journey together, you realize everyone here is also a part of your community. You may consider this group an extended part of your community or you may consider it close. Either way, at the end of the day, we're in each other's corners, and, more importantly, so is God.

Wrapping Up

Throughout this week, pray that God gives you the heart to see others the way He sees them and to love others the way He loves them. Pray that He will place a godly community in your life and that He will reveal to you ways to help transform your current community.

CHALLENGE: Make the effort to connect with at least two members of your community one-on-one this week!

Processing with God

Week 7: Intimacy with God

Week 8: Renewing Your Mind

Week 9: Lament

Week 7: Intimacy with God

Check-In Question:

How has living with your community affected your mental health over this past week?

Read John 15:1-8

Reflect

When this teaching was taking place, Jesus was speaking to his disciples—the people who had chosen to give up their entire lives to follow Him. Jesus clearly tells them that in order for their lives to remain fruitful they must remain in Him, and they did this by nurturing their relationship and building intimacy with Him.

Now I'm sure you're wondering how you can build and maintain a relationship with someone that you can't see and can't (always) hear. We may not be able to talk to God face-to-face like we can with our friends or family, but we can still connect with Him!

How do you connect with God?

_____

_____

_____

_____

_____

_____

_____

_____

_____

_____

_____

_____

_____

_____

There are so many different ways to connect with God! Now that you've heard how the rest of the group connects with God, what is a new way you want to try to connect with God?

_____

_____

_____

_____

_____

_____

_____

_____

God gives us two very clear ways to connect with Him: scripture and prayer. These are the two means of connection that most people associate with God, and each one is so important. We are told in 2 Timothy 3:14-17:

> *"But as for you, continue in what you have learned and have become convinced of, because you know those from whom you learned it, and how from infancy you have known the Holy Scriptures, which are able to make you wise for salvation through faith in Christ Jesus. All Scripture is God-breathed and is useful for teaching, rebuking, correcting and training in righteousness, so that the servant of God may be thoroughly equipped for every good work."*

When it says that all scripture is God-breathed that means it is inspired by God. God took the time to communicate the specific truths He wanted all of His people to know, and because of that blessing, we have the blessing of getting a glimpse into the heart of the Father. Through scripture, we can clearly see His heart for those He has created, His values, and His story. When we look at scripture, we get a chance to know the creator of everything deeper. Sometimes we step away from getting into the word because we can't feel a change when we're reading it. I'll ask you the same question one of my mentors asked me: "When you eat food, can you feel your body absorbing the nutrients it needs?"

We get the opportunity to know God deeper through prayer as well. There are three ways to connect with God in prayer: asking, abiding, and lamenting. Engaging in "asking prayer" is when we approach God with a list of things we would like to see happen. There is nothing wrong with asking God for these things, but if our only way of engaging with Him is through asking Him for things, how close can we really be? For example, if you had a friend who only ever contacted you when they needed something—even if it was something for someone else—how would that friendship make you feel? This is why abiding prayer is so important; abiding prayer is when we just sit and rest in God's presence. We can do this by thanking Him or just sitting in silence and listening for His voice. The last type of prayer we'll be focusing on is lamenting prayer. When we lament, we are processing our grief with God. We'll focus on this more in Week 9.

How would you describe your prayer life?

_____

_____

_____

_____

_____

_____

_____

_____

_____

_____

_____

I think many people would say they have active prayer lives, but we must evaluate how much of our prayer life is spent asking God for things versus thanking Him and listening for His voice. How would you feel if you had someone in your life that only came to you when they needed your help? They don't take the time to listen to you or get to know you, but you are always one of their first calls when they need help. Would you consider this person a friend? Probably not! Why would we expect different with our relationship with God? Why are we so often okay with playing this role for the King of Kings?

When Jesus shows us how to pray in the Lord's prayer (Matthew 6:9-13), half of the prayer is praise to God:

> *"Our Father in Heaven, hallowed be your name, your kingdom come, your will be done, on earth as it is in Heaven."*

We should model our own prayers like this as well. The more we sit with God in prayer and listen, the more familiar we become with His voice.

Take the remainder of the time to write a prayer to the Lord, remember not only to ask but give thanks and abide as well.

_____

_____

_____

_____

_____

_____

_____

_____

_____

_____

_____

_____

_____

_____

_____

_____

_____

_____

_____

_____

_____

_____

_____

_____

_____

_____

Wrapping Up

Throughout the next week, document changes you see occur in your prayer life!

- Pray for a hunger for God

- Pray that God makes Himself known to you

> *"Rejoice always, pray continually, give thanks in all circumstances; for this is God's will for you in Christ Jesus."*
>
> —1 Thessalonians 5:16-18

Week 8: Renewing Your Mind

Check-in question:

How has your prayer life changed over the past week? What new ways did you connect with God?

Read Romans 12: 1-2

Reflect

Our thoughts are important. They determine how we see others, they define our self-identity and self-worth, they are behind each and every decision we make. Our thoughts become our actions. When we become followers of God and offer ourselves to Him as a living sacrifice, who we are is drastically changed. We are made clean. Our minds are renewed, but what does that mean? As we walk further and further with God, not only can our thought-life change, it must.

Thoughts can be life-giving or life-taking. The enemy often tries to attack us in our thought-life, hoping we'll mistake lies for truth. The negative thoughts the enemy plants in your mind are a way to distract you.

What are some of the thoughts that frequently pop into your head? Positive and negative.

_____

_____

_____

_____

_____

_____

_____

_____

_____

_____

_____

_____

_____

_____

_____

_____

How have negative thoughts impacted your life, relationships, and faith?

_____

_____

_____

_____

_____

_____

_____

_____

_____

_____

Our thought patterns play a huge part in how we live our lives, and if our thoughts are not similar to His, we cannot live our life to the extent that He has called us to. God has commanded us to "take our thoughts captive," which means that when we partner with Him, we have the ability to change the way we think. The first step to changing our thought patterns is to recognize unhealthy thought patterns. To help you out, here's a quick guide[6]:

Thought Pattern	Explanation	Example
All-or-Nothing Thinking/ "Black and White" Thinking	Judging everything in absolutes, there is only black and white, no gray, any flaw makes the effort a total failure	"I was really anxious today, even though I thought I made progress. I'm not doing any better than I was before."
Overgeneralization	Seeing patterns based on one event	"I have had a terrible morning, so the rest of today is going to be awful."
Mental Filter	Only paying attention to evidence that affirms our thoughts/specific evidence	Sally always focuses on her failures and ignores moments she is successful.
Jumping to Conclusions: Mind Reading	Deciding what others are thinking without any evidence	"He didn't respond to me fast enough, he must not like me."
Jumping to Conclusions: Fortune-Telling	Predicting that the future will be bad without any evidence	"I know no matter how hard I try, I will never be good at this."
Emotional Reasoning	Assuming that our feelings point to facts	"I feel uncomfortable, so I must not be safe."
Creating Expectations	Creating expectations for yourself and others by using "should" and "must." This creates standards that will often not be fulfilled leading to frustration.	"You should have known I wouldn't like that."
Labeling	Putting labels on ourselves and others.	"I'm worthless." "He's a moron."
Personalization	Taking responsibility for/blaming yourself for something that was not entirely your fault. The flip side is accusing others and putting all the blame on them.	"My team lost the game because I missed a free throw."

6 The President and Fellows of Harvard College . (n.d.). *Identifying Negative Automatic Thought Patterns.* Harvard University Stress & Development Lab. Retrieved April 12, 2022, from https://sdlab.fas.harvard.edu/cognitive-reappraisal/identifying-negative-automatic-thought-patterns

Which of these negative thought patterns do you struggle with the most?

_____

_____

_____

_____

_____

_____

_____

_____

2 Corinthians 10:3-5 tells us:

> *"For though we walk in the flesh, we are not waging war according to the flesh. For the weapons of our warfare are not of the flesh but have divine power to destroy strongholds. We destroy arguments and every lofty opinion raised against the knowledge of God, and take every thought captive to obey Christ..."*

It may seem impossible to change the way we think, but that's not true. We have weapons that go beyond the power of the flesh. If we slow down and catch ourselves in negative thought patterns, we can replace the negative thought with a positively framed thought. The enemy tries to attack us by getting into our heads and making us believe lies that are not true. Rejecting negative thought patterns and thoughts that don't align with God's truth are ways that we can fight against the enemy. When something threatens our peace, we are able to combat it with God's truth.

When capturing negative thoughts, think of it as a 5-step process.

1. **Recognize:** What was the negative thought?
2. **Root:** What was the fear behind the thought?
3. **Identify:** Which negative thought pattern did you engage in?
4. **Truth:** What truth can bring you peace at this time?
5. **Reframe:** What is your reframed positive thought?

Here's an example:

Recognize	Root	Identify	Truth	Reframe
"My friends didn't invite me to the party. They must not like me anymore."	Rejection	Jumping to Conclusions: Mind Reading	I am chosen and loved by God.	"Even in moments I feel alone, I am still chosen and loved."

This next week, challenge yourself to take note of when a negative thought comes into your mind using the same framework. Let's start by filling the first row of this chart out with your most recurring negative thought.

Wrapping Up

Pray the following over yourself throughout the next week and try your best to take every thought captive!

- Do not let negative thoughts determine the outcomes in my life.

- Give me a heart that can focus on the silver lining.

Root	Recognize	Identify	Truth	Reframe

Week 9: Lament

Check-In Question:

How has the change in your thought patterns impacted your life? Were you more aware of the lies of the enemy?

Read Lamentations 3

Reflect

The book of Lamentations is a reflection on the Babylonian siege of Israel and the fall of Jerusalem (2 Kings 24-25). And in this book of the Bible, the author is vocalizing his grief over these events. To lament means to mourn or a "passionate expression of grief or sorrow." Throughout the book, the author vocalizes and processes his suffering and grief to God.

Do you feel comfortable bringing your emotions to God? Why or why not?

_____

_____

_____

_____

_____

Many of us grew up feeling as though we could not approach God in a way that expresses our hurt and disappointment, but this is not what the Bible indicates at all. It is okay for us to be unhappy with the cards we have been dealt and want to express that to God. In fact, it's biblical to do so! There are several chapters of lament (Job 3; Psalm 10, 63, 69, 74, 79) throughout the Bible, and God values lament so much that there is an entire book of the Bible devoted to it!

Lamenting is a means for us to healthily grieve and process our emotions with God. Whether these are feelings about a broken relationship, an unwanted diagnosis, or an unforeseen hardship, God wants to know what we're feeling and wants us to bring it to Him.

What is something you have been hesitant to bring before God?

_____

_____

_____

_____

_____

_____

_____

_____

_____

_____

Be honest with God about what you feel! Yes, He already knows, but when you bring it before Him, you're inviting Him to do healing work that He cannot perform if you are pretending that everything is okay. When we lament we're opening our hearts up to begin to heal, and it may hurt but it is for our greatest good. We can lament over our mental health struggles and be upset that we have to deal with them, and doing so does not make us any less faithful. In fact, it shows how faithful we are to come before the God of the universe and say, *"I don't like that I'm dealing with this, but if this is what you have for me I will use it for your glory."*

When we grieve we typically go through seven stages[7]:

1. Shock & Denial: The numb feeling that occurs after a loss/traumatic event
4. Pain & Guilt: An intense pain that comes after the shock wears off
5. Anger & Bargaining: Our pain turns to anger and may result in us trying to negotiate with ourselves or God to change the event that has occurred
6. Depression, Reflection, Loneliness: Sad reflection that occurs as the magnitude of the event sets in
7. The Upward Turn: Life becomes calmer as you begin to adjust
8. Reconstruction & Working Through: Realistic solutions begin to seem possible
9. Acceptance & Hope: You learn to accept and deal with your reality and have learned how to cope

Each of these stages offers its own challenges, but what is most important is for us to feel these feelings as we experience them rather than trying to pretend that everything is good. When we refuse to let ourselves process, we stay stuck in that place of hurt for much longer than we need to be.

Are you in the grieving process? If so, which stage are you in?

_____

_____

_____

_____

_____

_____

How can you invite God into your grief with you?

_____

_____

_____

_____

_____

7 http://socialworktech.com/2012/11/13/the-seven-stages-of-grief/

_____

_____

_____

_____

_____

_____

_____

As this group comes to an end formally, it is important that we understand how to process with God on our own. This can be done through prayer or writing in a journal, however you feel most comfortable sharing your heart with God.

Write a lament to God about whatever you are currently grieving. Be completely honest and vulnerable.

_____

_____

_____

_____

_____

_____

_____

_____

_____

_____

_____

_____

_____

_____

_____

_____

_____

_____

_____

_____

_____

_____

_____

_____

_____

_____

Wrapping Up

As you leave this group, actively invite God into the moments when you are processing your emotions. Pray the following:

- Ask God to allow you to experience your emotions fully.

- Speak honestly with Him about how you're feeling.

- Express your emotions however you need—crying is okay.

Our Goodbye

I am thankful for your bravery and all the effort you have put into this study. You have dived deeper into understanding yourself and, more importantly, God. The end of this group does not mean that the work is finished. On the contrary, the work has just begun. You are now open to everything the Lord wants to do inside your heart and mind. Let Him move however He sees fit.

More & More

Therapy, Medication, & the Church

Sometimes in the church, going to therapy or taking medication for your mental illness is stigmatized. This stigma comes from the flawed belief that if you struggle with these things then you are not trusting God enough. We would never say the same for physical illnesses, so why would we treat mental illnesses any different? A cancer patient is not shamed for engaging in chemotherapy, and the standard should be the same for a person dealing with a mental illness utilizing therapy or medicine. You have nothing to be ashamed of if you take part in either of these things. Medication and therapy are wonderful tools that God helped people create so that they are on an even playing field with everyone else. Neither of these methods indicate that you do not trust God enough, it is you using the tools He has provided you with so that you can partner with Him in the healing process. Jesus can work through therapy and medicine in order to walk us through our healing process. If these tools are what works best for you, allow yourself to take part in these gifts as you embark with the Lord on your healing journey.

If you have ever felt shame for using these tools, take the time to write a prayer asking God to release you from the shame. Shame never comes from God, it comes from the enemy.

_____

_____

_____

5-4-3-2-1 Coping

The 5-4-3-2-1 coping technique is one of the top grounding techniques recommended by therapists for those experiencing panic attacks.

Start by focusing on taking slow deep breaths—5 seconds in, 5 seconds out. Use this as a way to regulate your breathing. Once your breathing is fully regulated, begin the countdown:

5: Find **five** things that you can see surrounding you. Big or small. Focus on anything around you that helps remind you where you are.

4: Find **four** things around you that you can touch. Touch them. Notice the texture and how it feels below your fingertips.

3: Listen and identify **three** things you can hear.

2: Notice **two** smells.

1: Notice **one** thing you can taste, what does the inside of your mouth taste like at this moment?

Other Helpful Grounding Techniques

The following techniques are not step-by-step processes, but they are great simple ways to ground yourself after a panic attack.

- Splash water on your face or run water over your hands

- Stomp your feet on the ground

- Wiggle your fingers and toes

- Complete a puzzle or play a game

- Listen to comforting music

- Hug someone you love

- Journal about your feelings

All of these techniques are not for everyone, but you can use the ones that fit you best to ground you back into the present.

More on Suicide

The Warning Signs

- Withdrawing from family and friends

- Increased drug and alcohol use

- Saying goodbye to loved ones

- Impulsive or reckless behavior

- Aggressive behavior

- Dramatic mood swings

- Giving away personal possessions

- Check-in with family and friends; many people who are struggling with suicidal thoughts don't want to come forth for fear of burdening others.

- Express support and concern

- Do not argue or raise your voice—be patient

- If you think a loved one is considering suicide, ask direct questions:

- "Do you have a plan to hurt yourself?"

- "What you've said leads me to believe you are considering suicide. Do you have a plan to end your life?"

If you or someone you know is in an emergency, call 911 or go to an emergency room immediately!

Contacts

- Suicide and Crisis Lifeline: 988 (Call or SMS)

- If you're uncomfortable talking on the phone you can text 741-741 to be connected to a free trained crisis counselor on the Crisis Text Line. Visit https://www.crisistextline.org/ for more information.

About the Author

Cameron Pace is an author, mental health advocate, and student at Asbury Theological Seminary pursuing her Master of Arts in Ministry.

She is passionate about bringing conversations concerning mental health to the forefront of the church, as well as connecting individuals that need help with the proper resources. She desires reconciliation for those who have been hurt by the church due to the stigmas that surround mental health.

She graduated from the University of Georgia with a bachelor's degree in special education. While obtaining her undergraduate degree, she was able to student teach at Jefferson Middle School and several other schools at the K-12 level. Teaching helped her learn more about how she could use her teaching gift along with her faith and knowledge of mental health to help those around her. The experiences ultimately inspired her to write this book.

She continues to live in Athens, Georgia working with college-aged students through the University of Georgia Wesley Foundation, and she is a dog mom to her miniature schnauzer, Ducky.

www.ingramcontent.com/pod-product-compliance
Lightning Source LLC
Chambersburg PA
CBHW041517120626
46551CB00018B/2471